BEATING THE GRAVES

BEATING
THE GRAVES

Tsitsi Ella Jaji

University of Nebraska Press / Lincoln and London

Acknowledgments for the use of copyrighted
material appear on page 97, which constitutes
an extension of the copyright page.

The African Poetry Book Series has been made
possible through the generosity of philanthropists
Laura and Robert F. X. Sillerman, whose
contributions have facilitated the establishment
and operation of the African Poetry Book Fund.

Library of Congress Cataloging-
in-Publication Data
Names: Jaji, Tsitsi, author.
Title: Beating the graves / Tsitsi Ella Jaji.
Description: Lincoln: University of Nebraska
Press, [2017] | Series: African Poetry Book series
Identifiers: LCCN 2016034814 (print)
LCCN 2016041951 (ebook)
ISBN 9780803299603 (softcover: acid-free paper)
ISBN 9781496200112 (epub)
ISBN 9781496200129 (mobi)
ISBN 9781496200136 (pdf)
Classification: LCC PS3610.A385
A6 2017 (print) | LCC PS3610.A385
(ebook) | DDC 811/.6—dc23
LC record available at https://
lccn.loc.gov/2016034814

Set in Garamond Premier by Rachel Gould.

for Franklin D. Cason Jr.

in lingering embrace

CONTENTS

BEATING THE GRAVES

ANKESTRAL.

Drought

It is so goddamn hot in our country that blooms
               —jacarandas, bougainvilleas, flamboyants—
erupt in a shock of fuchsia from pipes laced with rust.
Hokoyo! Step too close and your skin will crisp up like a chicken in hot Olivine.
          Everyone will see the fat sizzling from your innards.
It is so hot that locusts
drop in pools around your feet,
their musical legs all melted.

In our nation a waterfall is a cauldron of steaming falsehoods.

        S m o k e   t h u n d e r s . . .

Maize simply withers in
the miserly shade of thorns.
Men quiver at cock's crow and
hang their cattle out to dry.

      Pumpkins turn to gourds.
      Midnight flushes out hunger.
      Ngozi dart in disregard
      across the oozing tar.

Ach man, spare us your sermons
concerning our weeknight brews:
the problem we are facing now
is the drunkard who drains
his own water pot, leaving
the mother of his children

with one thing only:
                pure grit.

                        Rhinos are shrinking.
                        Filthy crawfish bloat.
                        Our grandmother is just seated
                        as if death were a bus running late.

We have now reached the stage
where lackeys are openly trafficking
dragon fruit, smuggling them through
customs as if they were Marange diamonds.
Meanwhile, at the small house,
their scrawny young girlfriends
are just hassling the houseboys.

Our eyes run
all through October,
slash-and-burnt
like rhizomes.

We hear the drum's skin
crackling as it curls.
We smell the coming rain.
Archangel, your time draws near.

The Book of VaNyemba

Ex nihilo, omnia.

a
hill
of beans

I missed Sekuru's funeral. Only the stranger who was my aunt
was left to condole. Across the oceanic hiss of telephone static,

twenty years thick, Baba repeated my flight number.
To get them talking again, Sekuru died.

When I arrived she said I was her twin.
I wondered why she had not missed me.

How do I bury the shame of not knowing which tree to turn after
for the road—such as it is—to their land, *kumusha*?

We rode in the new uncle's pickup truck to the farm. Whining
in the backseat about his open beer bottle, I was scared.

I was scared of going *kumusha* without Sekuru,
scared I would not have the words for his grave,

scared to walk his fields,
scared I would forget which cows he'd given me,

scared that now he was gone, no one would gather us under the kitchen
thatch to kneel, and clap for protection, and take snuff with the ancestors.

I am right. Kneeling at his graveside,
I have no words to bring him back.

Virgines eius squalidæ, et ipsa oppressa amaritudine.

Tete sits me down and tells me the story of our ankestors.
She says it with a hard K. I squelch my sass, and listen.

Our ankestors were hunters, of the zebra totem.
There were two brothers and a very beautiful sister,
as sweet as a sugar bean. So they called her VaNyemba.

They came all the way from Mozambique to this place,
tracking wild game. When the chief saw VaNyemba's beauty,
he granted her brothers leave to hunt on his land.

They set out to hunt early, leaving VaNyemba to tend the fire.
She was very beautiful.   The chief surprised her.
She screamed, but her brothers were far, far.

He was a heavy man, and as he thrust himself inside her
he found her penis. Our VaNyemba hanged her busted bare
body. When the chief saw it, he was afraid. He stripped

off his regalia and fled, leaving the land to her brothers.
That is the land they buried her in. And that is how
we came to live in Chihota, the land of sweet potatoes.

I am sitting next to Tete, wondering if
I will ever eat a sweet potato again.

Alia autem ceciderunt in petrosa, ubi non habebant terram multam.

take.
eat.

this land
is your land.

this land was given
for my body.

this
mangled body.

this land was handed
over to you.

kings and kingdoms
          passed away.
this is my body. this land was broken
over my dead body.

tend it.
tend it.

—till this land—
          your land.

Benedictus fructus ventris tui.

ground
nuts.

field
peas.

black eye
peas.

split
pea
cow
pea
chick
pea.
kidney.
pinto.
red. red

lentil.
yellow
lentil.
nyimo.
navy.
garbanzo.

buttah
bean.
lima
bean.
green
bean.

salt.
pea
nut.
salt
pea
nuts.

sugah
bean, honey.

nyemba.
vanyemba.

Esurivi enim, et dedistis mihi manducare

Come, let us eat.
Ngatidyei.

Come, let us pray:
Ngatirumbidzei:

Our Grandmother, VaNyemba, we bless you.
Makaita basa, VaNyemba, Ambuya vedu.

Grandmother, we sing your name in the fields and in the mountains.
Ambuya, tinorumbidza zita renyu muminda ne mumakomo.

You died for your land, but you were victorious. Praises, Grandmother, high praises.
Imi mafirenyika yenyu, munorumbidzwa nemupururu Ambuya

Give us this day plenty of sweet potatoes.
Tipei mangwanani ano zvihota zvakarasirira.

O, how we rejoice to eat your sweet potatoes.
Nemupururu tinoda kudya mbambaira yenyu.

And how we love to eat your sugar beans.
Tinopembera kudya mutakunanzva waVaNyemba.

For we are your great grandchildren, raised at your breast;
Tisu, tiri vazukuruzukuru venyu yakayamwa musvisvinwa waVaNyemba;

Yes, we come from the Land of Sweet Potatoes.
Hongu, kumusha kwedu ndekwaChihota.

Praise be, Sweet Sugar Bean
Mupururu kwamuri, VaNyemba.[1]

1. After having lived abroad for two decades, my ability to express myself in Shona has faltered. The struggle towards language is not solitary. I thank my father, Lazarus Jaji, for lending me his poetic ear. We write ourselves together.

Eli, Eli, lamma sabacthani? hoc est: Deus meus, Deus meus ut quid dereliquisti me?

On the third day of the hunt, our sister.
On the third day of the hunt, our sistren.
On the third day of the hunt, our mother who wert called hermaphrodite.

On the third day, our intersex ancestor.
On the third day, our intersex ankestor, hallowed be thy name.
On the third day, our intersex ankestor, how wouldst thou have
    wished to be called?

Wouldst thou have recognized our stories
—bullets in the wallet of your womb?
Wouldst thou, our splendid sister, have been happier hunting as a brother?

Our beginning, you who were robbed of your self, what could have
comforted you, soothed your terror, eased your tender, tender heart?
What would you have wanted to hear us whisper, your name, your
truth, your home? What would have broken your search for woven
vine-rope?

Our blessed third-gender ancestor, how shall we summon you?

Oculi tui columbarum, absque eo, quod intrinsecus latet.

O Daddy Rex,
you horn-billed bronze.

Shake that mane, baby,
flash that strobe-colored coat.

Dazzle us, old Guinea-Eyes,
all black and white and
red all over.

Let me hear you
do that *njenjenje*,
you earth rambler, you.

Kick up a storm, sweetheart.
Kick with your mouth.

You, highway-robbed of
you, endless gift.

***

Praise Song for Patricia Jabbeh Wesley

Oyehe heeeeeeh. MotherPoet!
Your fatha taught you to be bold.
If something is true, keep doing it.
Ah, you, Doctor Patricia Jabbeh Wesley!
You are the mother of four children.
Mama Wesley, you have raised
four black human beings in this thicket called
America. You, Grebo woman. You
have
done
well.
You have raised four human beings
in this thicket of words
and wordless slights.

Ah, who can say you are timid?
Who can say you do not know how to throw your voice into the air?
And who would have pushed that air aside, if not for you?
Who has come to the door asking for Liberian womanspeak poetry?
Hehnnnn, they want to know, who is listening-o?

Ayi! Patricia Jabbeh Wesley, we are standing
on your shadow. Forgive us, mother.
We have been crowing like johnny-come-latelies:
Maonaka? Ndasvika panyika iyi nemakumbo angu, ndega.
What! We are saying what?
That
we
have
arrived?
Is it?

But who made a shelf for us?
Aiwa, tiri tese!
Who micro-braided her own hair
and blocked the TV screen, a MamiWata for today
hands perched on her child-bearing hips?
Who put the pepper pot down
hard, there, in the middle of the table,
ready to spar joke for joke,
ready to match these men?

Did you hear the one about the Ibgo, the Yoruba, the Hausa,
and the mango tree?
Aho!
But what of the Yoruba, the Hausa, and the Igbo who jumped off the roof?
Hehnnn.
Ah, you, Patricia.
What kind of people joke about those who have died very hard?

But you look death in the eye and it looks down.
You look death in the eye and you weep,
then take off your glasses to look at us straight on.
You look death in the eye, burying your sister's children,
and your teacher's teachers. You do the woman's part.
You refuse to wail. You will not be quiet.
Even we who are very very small
would like to be like you.

We want to have your accent.
We want to make people work
hard for our words.

We want our voice to have your husk.
We want to inform people at
the other tables who were not

even eavesdropping at all, at all
that we are not Kriyo . . .
Hehnnn.
We are not Kriyo.

We want the buttons on our wool blazers to strain hard like that.
We want to wear red frames like yours. That same rectangle shape.
We want to take off those glasses again, to weep for joy at
our young sister-upstarts. We want to hehnnn like that.
We want to dent the table of conversation with the
struggle that is *us*. It is not easy-o.
Four books of poetry,
four children, and
an African Husband.
Hehnnn.

Patricia. You are your fatha's daughter.
We thank him for teaching you to take up space,
but we thank you for standing in that space.
We thank you for pushing the word *no* so hard it fell backward.
We thank you for squeezing the word *man* so tight it noticed
it was missing two very important letters.
We thank you for pushing the point.
We are inviting you now.
We are saying
Mother Patricia, teach us.
We are not ready to become big women like that.
We are not ready to make sure that our uncles
are buried properly. We are not ready
to learn how. But watching you,
we just did.

If something is true, keep doing it.

Song of Yobe

Introit for Girls' Voices: In the Physics Lab

Fire. We flinch, then lean in to the light.
A Bunsen burner transfigures air
into flickering tongues of indigo.
We watch the curious commotion
of copper sulfate flaring into
a bright blaze of turquoise.

Fire. We come to learn how compressed air
powers an engine, how pressure does work.
We come to prove our candlelit diligence,
our memories sharpened by flame.
What we know cannot be countered—the law of
thermodynamics, relativity, force.

Open the gates and examine us.
We will silence those city bureaucrats who claim
girls who learn by firelight will never pass. Tomorrow
we do our part. We wield our nibbled pens
for the principle of uncertainty.
Our heads are clear, our minds made up.

Antiphon for Boys' Voices: In Sambiza Forest

Fire. First the sour smell
of petrol spilt on dust.
We too knew of conversion:
chemical energy turning to light.
We were slow. But clutched in flames,
we wasted all their bullets, charred as we were.

Ashen, now we spirit-see the mad one leap
from a lorry. She limps into the dead
of night. More sober, her sisters take to
the forest. They cook, they pray, they pray again.
Our sooty eyes foresee their return, nursing
horrors at their breast, fired,

fired with impossible love.
Look at us, we twenty-nine
boys gone up in smoke. Bring us back
to mind. Water our memory
with your tears.
O, spare us some water too.

To Praise the Hornbill

for Chris Abani (after Harryette Mullen)

Splatter-winged nutcracker.
Crick-cracking horn honker.
Crunk-billed golden nester.
Hoot, you hungry seersucker.

Sunny-side: Calypso Kitchen.
Smack-tongued, seedy toaster trash.
Yellowbeak roosted raunch,
crank-pot slow and conched.

Button down those breastplates.
Platter plenty of tinny,
Guinea spotted dick. Strut
wing-tipped through the ball.

Blitz! Calling all dapple-
blacked, war-painted, slick-
downed root doctors. Wing
it, baby, wing it.

O stray dusted hornbill,
eye-twinkler. What a
swingin' life you've lushed.
Evolved? Hell no. Elevated.

Deep English

Walk through the edges,
circumvent the center.
(Circle the square, so to speak).

Having parted ways with the crossroad,
take each path offered, and unite into
a thousand thousand fragments.

Stutter in the tongues of men and angels.
Spit out the honorific truth:
rave stark as a mad woman.

Destitute, discover the ankestral home
and sit down to fast sumptuously
at the high table.

Comforted, stare into the mirror
that divided all these years,
the mirror that melts in the mouth.

Now, speak clearly.

BOTANICAL.

The Go-Betweens

Mai's bridewealth:
a letter of resignation to the board of missions;
duplicates to supporting congregations;
two plane tickets; two ceremonies; two receptions, one large.
Being American, her family made no further claims.
Neither did her adopted Manyika brothers.

*

Grandpa's wedding gift to Mai and Baba:
one piano and two pecan trees.
Chickens were barbecued. Fish were caught.

*

The bridewealth of Mainini Fay, Mai's Manyika sister:
various beasts, cash, and goods, up to and including furniture and a fridge,
to which Mai objected, shaming their brothers.
Said fridge was deducted, but remains in the accounts of the saga.

*

The bridewealth for my young brother's bride-to-be:
given as calves to him at age four. Slighted, I raised cane
and also got a few. The cows stayed on the farm, *kumusha*.
Babamunini counted, corralled, herded, nursed, milked, cleaned,
prodded, yoked, and slaughtered them. So, ask him if you need to know
which ones are which, or when they died.

*

My bridewealth: a helicopter
engraved on a collector's coin
to tickle my father. Stateside,
my brother had no need of cows.

*

The bridewealth of my grandmother, Ambuya:
unsecured. When her husband died, and again when she was gone,
this was factored into the burial ceremonies as fines to be paid in goats.
And MoneyGrams.

*

Baba built that house for Ambuya and Sekuru with his first paycheck.
Bricks and mortar with a shiny metal roof.
When he married, Mai helped him
fill it with store-bought sofas covered in knots of bumpy wool
and green melamine plates. Plus, there was a wood-burning iron stove
locked up in the kitchen built of bricks. Ambuya kept the key on string
around her waist. It was never used once.

*

And so, I moneygram the bridewealth owed by Babamunini, my uncle,
who is my small father by virtue of being the younger brother to my father.
Babamunini, who beat his own mother once
when his medication ran out.
Forgive me, Mainini, my future little mother.
My mental math tells me you will outlive him.

Family Trees.

mother was a mango transplanted by moonlight. she glowed like spilt cream. on unknown days she would burst into bruises, or leak tears, but it was just a skin game. fruit do that, seeping out ripe-juice, when inside all is sweetening. the real hurt was slower, deeper.

as the years swelled, her tenderness rooted in the soil of dented fruit. the real rage was churned with the fatherwomen. then they hurled it together like paint at uncles gouging *lobola* or marrying twice or taunting children.

these days everyone is quieter as she begins to sag into the third age, so terribly afraid of going blind.

brother was a flamboyant tree. he arrived like flint and steel, which we fought over until everyone died. at first he would run through the house bass-booming for us to wake up. but as it became clear to him that no one would dye his room red he settled down to chewing gum and playing foosball.

now, once a week, he hands out pocket money, backwards.

we are so proud of him.

father, an acacia, was exactly the same only, before brother hustled
steel, he herded cattle. he handed out proverbs with a largess
too tardy to make anyone fluent. there was always a tangle of
thornwire barbed under his skin.

i cannot remember the history of the scars, except to know that it
was our own uncles who lit the fire.

the acacia survives immolation.
the acacia screeches with laughing children.
the acacia cries like a man, pregnant with meaning.

the sister is tough. she is dropping frangipani blossoms on the soil-red plot while things fall apart. her ivory bloodlets are the inverse of the mother's. everything is chilled, yet she gives off a scent as if, within her, rocks were smoldering.

she is a locked bowl of bee's gold.

she is equally silent,
equally flammable.

we call that aunt a **fatherwoman**. A boarding school master
could snatch her branches to strip them for caning. hunted, hers
was a hard wood. *mopane,* or *mukwa* perhaps. it emerges that she
is remembering a pendulated body, the rape of the royal house of
zebra, the lustfear that drove the brute away, and the winning of
the land for sweet potato cultivation like it was yesterday.

she plucks away at her bearded chaos.

who can count the mouths she feeds?

there is an **"uncle."** how can i put it? some claim he gripped us like an unplanted vine.

yet the fact is, water is better than blood when one is thirsty. and all those years there were sister-brother fruits on the table when the in-laws were spoiling. and everyone had enough. for the moment, it is better to keep still and plan on grapes some other time. let's,

let's stay together.

some things hold a mirror to the earth, as with this recent
grandmother and simultaneously, her **fathergrand-uncle**. he was
wide and whorled, and just as empty as a cream-of-tartar fruit.
she was wiry and wizened like national baobab roots. together
they met at the drought: the corruptions, the lamentations. they
tapped morse code across the ocean for years, detailing pickup
trucks, bags of maize, longing.

one day they stopped haggling and ate a goat
and we all went back to dying peacefully.

look, the **cousin-brothers** grow like weeds, to put it bluntly.
the fatherwoman wants to pull them all up by their rude little
groundnuts. but look at it this way. this is a drought. and the field is
all that stands between us and a hollowed rectangle.

consider the cuts, the aches, and the sun-lash we take to salvage a
single pumpkin plant. at the end of the day, it is three feasts in one:
leaves and gourd flesh and blooming "tomatoes."

or take the eucalyptus, growing more stubborn each time we mow it down.
nevertheless, how well it clears our throat.

***

Vindication

They used to call it Murdertown, USA.

There was once a whole wall of my people
in the gym at Austintown-Fitch. Then
rust belted America down and steel sock-hopped
out of Youngstown on two left feet.

*

One time, the band teacher said,
You have more talent in your little pinky
than she has in her entire body.
But she *practices.*

*

They were Ethels, and Nellies, and Mary Ellas, and Lils;
fruit-farmers, dress-makers, and sometimes squirrel-hunters.
Next it was four rounds of
Hoover, Hoover, vacuum cleaner.

*

Clarence spent my Grandpa Bill's tuition on a brand-new Cadillac.
About that time, Grandma watched her uncle George
go up in a plane and come right back down,
dead.

*

One thing Mary Ella always remembered,
even after she couldn't, was how Uncle George
picked her peck of strawberries
so she could go to the picnic.

*

The scent of Florida water used to roll off Grandpa Bill's brow.
It clung to his golf shirt till the direct sun
retired his whole entire wardrobe and dressed him up
as leather.

*

I used to steer from his shoulders,
kicking a scapula here,
tugging a tuft of white hair there.
Back then, I was blinkered to pain.

*

From Grandpa's shoulders you could see
clear to Ohio. Every night the condominium circle
played the same hand of pinochle
until Mary Ella was clean out of trump.

Holy Departure (A Berceuse)

for Sekuru Jaji

It is today, then.
The wrapping in blankets
and laying to rest
in your new cradle,
the earth.

How faithfully you tilled it,
shifting soil into mounds,
warming the beginnings of
sweet potatoes, spiny cucumbers,
pumpkins and groundnuts.

How often you patted the ground
with your small feet. How
you goaded the cattle on,
up the hills, across the granite,
in search of grass.

You laid out the traps
for mice and other delicacies
and snared bird after
haughty bird with a stone,
grounding Icarus.

Lay down and rest, dear one.
The others have been waiting for you.
Swaddled in soft colors,
sleep calmly,
knowing that we know

where you are resting,
where to find you.
We will sit by your side
and listen to your peaceful breath,
ever newly born.

Dust to Dust

There are women who have no rage left in their wrists.
They slice greens and skin tomatoes at the same time every day.
Their husbands are at the beer gardens just drinking
money—bottle after bottle of beans or margarine
or soap.

There are women who press lip to quiet lip,
as they brush a fly from their brow. They
swallow their own mucus in the chill. Or
vaguely wonder how love began or
when they became a commonplace.

Did they know when they were born
that a heart can turn into cinnamon dust,
that all that's involved is lipstick, unease,
roasted meat, and the cost of deodorant.

There are men condemned to stagger home
for the rest of their lives to fuck someone
who smells of kerosene. Someone who
will not preen and who wears long, brown dresses.
Someone who will rarely hurry across a busy road,

who moves as carefully as if
she were carrying a heap of rust.

Document for U.S. Citizens Who Have Never Applied for a Visa and Have Had It Up to Here with Those Loud Aliens Who Go On and On about Some Letter

It is not like going to the bank.

There are no hard candies in a basket made in China,
and no Kleenexes on the counter.
There is no refund if someone forgets to wish you a good day.

There are no chairs for the aged,
no toys for two-year-olds with earaches,
no supervisor to speak to in case of the
Absurd.

There are no meal vouchers if it takes all day,
no list of local hotels with a negotiated rate.
No one wants to know if you are a doctor.

Plastic is not magic. Seals are not signs.
Your cousin-brother's wedding is not relevant.
Hell, there is no such thing as a cousin-brother.

And it is always your fault: not enough planning,
the wrong color passport, the misplaced stress
in a word.

Blunt Balm

The balm
of Gilead
will heal
will shrink
will shrug
off the
losses. Profits
made elsewhere
means that
$300 for a bottle of the pills in India,
less for improv. Hepcats could lay it on ya . . .
$10 a day or less for Sovaldi.
That's 1%. Not the.
That's 1% of what it costs for the Balm in Gilead.
Baby baby baby baby Babylon.
By the river baby lay me down down Babylon chaunt.
Gilead can blunt criticism concerning 91/half/less/millions.
Less than. Less grumbling. Less mumbling. Less never say
a word. A mumbling. Never said that. Never said a mumbling word.

Left behind: Brazil, China, Turkey.
Brazil nut.
China plate.
Turkey time.
Tackey. Tactless. The tactic is
less about money
and more blunt.
Less here,
more there.
Less is more, then.
130 million > 3 to 500,000.

As in: more than 130 million people are infected with the
hepatitis C virus, and 300,000 to 500,000 people die from
the infections each year, according to the World Health
Organization. Whoah. Like Ebola, lalalalala bamba. Bowling for
combined sales, lurid scenes, blood seeping.
It just doesn't make copy. Just cents on the dollar.

Malaria. Yawn. Hepatitis. Yawn. AIDS. Yawn.
On the other hand: STEM.
Eyes light up for math.
Eyes light up at math.
Eyes light up at the math.
Just do the math. Now
the wheels are spinning.
Big Money, big money
maker: The version of hepatitis C that is most prevalent in India
requires that patients take Sovaldi for 24 weeks, meaning that
they would need 6 bottles for a total cost of $1,800, Mr. Alton
said. Gilead will receive a royalty of 7% of sales of the generic
versions. Cha-ching 7 per 100 for 18 of those Benjamins. All
about the. 70 and 560 and cha-chingalingling. Dang. 630 in
his head, Mr. Alton said. Babam. Kazam. Badabang badaboo.
Besides. Sovaldi is on pace to become one of the world's top-
selling drugs, with more than $10 billion in sales this year. In the
U.S., a 12-week-supply costs $84,000, which
some
critics
say
is
too
high
for
a

life-
saving
drug.
Gilead says: dang, baby, it's cheaper than those treatments you
used to try, and they didn't even work, plus, dang, baby, its cheaper
than a liver transplant and dang this balm is 90% guaranteed
money back make you feel like a million bucks. Or somewhat
more balmy in 8 to 12 weeks.
90>60. Undeniably.
There is
a balm
in Gilead. To heal
the sickly/not all wounds can be made whole.
Made whole.
Made whole.

with assistance from the New York Times

Matobo Hills

Here lie the remains of Cecil Rhodes, Colossus:
landlocked, rock-clad in dolomite, as he willed it.

Cairo shrugged him off. The Cape had him removed.
Yet here Rhodes lies still, dead as a diamond.

No one digs him up. No one cries, *Bayete!*
This view   is wasted on him.

Philosophical Investigations

1. In which the poet posts a query to Facebook wondering which verb tense should be employed when referring to the subject as "comrade."

2. In which, as an academic specializing in English literature and, by extension, language, the poet might reasonably wonder about the key principles involved in this, or any other grammatical problem, after all.

3. In which the poet experiences a fear of crocodiles.

4. In which the poet notices that crocs appear to be a recurring theme, and then moves on.

5. In which the poet decides to confine wondering to the poem, rather than risk wandering into murky waters, and deletes the initial quandary.

6. In which the poet turned Afronaut embarks upon further exploration of the upper reaches of grammar as navigated by the Internet, tritely.

7. In which the poet consults perfect-english-grammar.com/verb -tenses.html.

8. In which the poet, compulsively checking Facebook, suddenly tenses upon discovering that her post has been triple-liked (well actually just liked by 3 people), checks to make sure that the original post has indeed been deleted, and notes with relief that it is simply the Africa Is a Country article about the ho-hum topic of South African xenophobia that has garnered said likes; these things resolved, the poet returns to the matter of higher grammatical constructions.

9. In which the poet reads: *How to make the tense.*

10. In which the poet considers what defines tension.

11. In which the poet again abandons monkey-mind, scolding her inner *mukanya*, that crafty baboon, and returns to the obvious.

12. In which the poet, being a zebra, takes satisfaction in the totemic aptness of sticking to black and white, reading between the lines, as it were.

13. In which, "tense," as it were, acquires use-value.

14. In which the original confusion is parsed, under cover: http://tinyurl.com/na5e35u.

15. In which the poet regrets how the use of a tinyurl obscures from view the full headline in which the choice phrase "bedroom coup" turns heads.

16. In which it is confirmed through revisiting the perplexing post which occasioned the foregoing prolegomenon that indeed, the chairperson referred to the expelled comrades as comrade so-and-so, comrade thus-and-such, comrade etcetera-etcetera, and comrade fill-in-the-blank, so to speak.

17. In which irony is noted, and a dead horse is beaten, such that those in doubt are assured that the comrades were named.

18. In which it is decided not to elaborate as to the irony of the comrade chairperson announcing news of the demise of a faction to which he had been believed to belong, and thus a Frank O'Hara move is made.

19. In which we return to the original question: which tense?

20. In which "I am a comrade" serves as an opening example, and a corresponding date, perhaps 1979, is suggested were one to draw up a table, where column A were to be labeled

"Example"; column B to be labeled "Simple Present"; and column C to be designated for corresponding dates.

21. In which, to avoid tedium, other persons, such as the second, third, pluralities, majorities, minorities, dissenting bodies, thus and such are abandoned, the table having been set up in the opening gestures.

22. In which

    a. I am being a comrade, playing fair and square, carrying my party card, singing my *chimurenga* songs, wearing my free T-shirt, and eating chicken;

    b. Present Continuous;

    c. 1980–

23. In which

    a. I have been a comrade;

    b. The Present is Perfectly Simple;

    c. 2006– (during which time I have been being a comrade, I assure you, this whole time, it was just that you were not able to ascertain this due to the fact that at that time you were not yet monitoring me, due, no doubt, to the many important and valuable activities you were engaged in, aspiring, attaining, and burnishing your excellence, see).

24. In which

    a. I was a comrade

    b. the past was simple

    c. it was dawn

25. In which past this seemed progressive.

26. In which I had been a comrade, the past had been perfect, and any and all criticisms in the present by the when-we's, the disaffected migrants, and the entire global north were taken to be insulting.

27. In which we break//The past has never been perfect.// Analogous to we have never been modern. A reference inserted to assure those whose reading habits tend toward the recursive and who may have momentarily referred back to Investigation Number 2, that indeed, the poet is trained in the discipline of literature, a field less concerned with works (and, as far as the vast majority is concerned, working) and more concerned with theory, such as systems.

28. In which I had been being a comrade, if you recall.

29. In which I will be a comrade later. Other examples include I will meet the comrade later. You will come to the comrade's house. It will rain tomorrow on the comrade's farm. She will be late planting, due to her responsibilities as an MP. He will help us later to file our papers, attesting to our membership in the comrade's brigade. We will get married in September—a ridiculous example given that history is now in its farcical stage. They will cook dinner for the comrade on his next and most excellent birthday, and for all birthdays thereafter, in perpetuity, and the angels and archangels will join in the feast, singing *Chimurenga One, Chimurenga Two, Chimurenga Three* and for evermore, monopolizing freedom in the great and glorious past, which was perfect, which—having been so rudely and homosexually interrupted by the English language, mining, tobacco, and various other machinations—will resume in the continuous tense known as the simple future.

30. In which it was not all bad, but neither was it any good.

31. In which it should also be clarified that the poet does not believe archangels are the only heavenly beings.

32. In which we note that the simple future tense is helpfully glossed on the well-designed and authoritative website as "(or future with will)."

33. In which the irony is noted, again.

34. In which an act of will returns us to the task at hand.

35. In which example one for the future continuous, "I will be sleeping" may seem apt to those readers finding this entire exercise to be one in tedium.

36. In which that is the whole point.

37. In which the poet navigates to the "Future Perfect Simple Form" and wishes to "Click here to learn about how to USE this tense" and, scrolling down further, considers that it would also be helpful to "Click here to learn about irregular past participles."

38. In which, for those somewhat confused, an example would be "I will have finished being comradely."

39. In which I will have been working out the tensile strength of the operations connoted by the use of that most flexible of subjects, the comrade.

40. In which *a luta continua.*

Limpopo Blues

I am not swimming across this river. I am reading a headline
in the free newspaper on the plane: *17 Zimbabweans drown in
Limpopo River.* I do not call my cousin-brothers in Cape Town
when I touch down in Jozi for the conference, in case they want
bus fare to come visit me, or sound flat when I mention my book,
or notice that I ask about their little one, but not by name. What
a croc, this river between rand and dollar, and neither one ours.
This river has double-crossed us.

Wait Until the Leader Clears the Lunar

after a sign seen in a SEPTA train tunnel in Philadelphia, PA

/Wait. /Stop.// Wait until the Lead_{sheet}?. ///Stop.///// **STOP!!!**
/All clear. /Stop./ Let the moon through. /Stop./

[Just Etymologic:]

> **regarding the moon** / *della luna:*
> –shine, shiny, ADJ. : *illuminato dall luna.*
> –struck, ADJ. : *lunatico, pazzo.*
> **moor**[1], TR.: *(nav.) gettare l'ancora ; dare*

but this is just moonshine talk
    throw that_[anchor]
    overboard.

> *From below, the*
> *meniscus frays.*

What is this thing called?

Diagnostics:

> *Tengo hambre.*
> *Tango, hombre,*
> *Tango africando—mayombé!*

What is this thing?

Now, Etiologic: Let us discuss this in the waiting room

Luna huyende.
Meniscal loons:
Mayombe—bombe—mayombé!

wailin'
wailin'

in the wailin' room

What is this?

The Symptom Attic   Sign|ifie(d/r)

lost sisters,

fools who take wing
into that waveless world where
nothing can breathe through its ribs.

Stop./Drop./Roll.
d/r feel good.

daughtah.

Clear your mind, colored
gyal.

just think about it for a second/
why would you toss your
anchor skyward except to
spend the rest
of your rainbows fleeing gravity,
as the moon does—
month in, month out.

Luminous Anthem, you electric flesh-fish!

> Why not spark your tentacles into
> a thousand stunted fingerstrands of
> light? Wait there, under the
> meniscus, and whisper the memo
> into my mouth. Underwaterwith.

Known Carcinogenics:
May the Great Leader always illuminate
the Upper Reaches of the Sunsquash Layercake,
the Heaven-Bound Eggs, and
the Cholesterol-Freed Golden Meringue.
> ***And the people said blasé.***
Let the Great Leader come through.
> ***Blasé.***
Let the Great Leader motorcade his way,
roughshod, across the navy swathes
until they are completely worn through,
bleached tight and bright.
> ***Blasé.***

Prognostic: Cassandra/VaNyemba/Nongqawuse

> *What is this thing called, love?*

> *This funny thing called*

il pazzo mio, il gran lunatico, il glorioso, furioso, e ludico!

> come through to me.

After the leader. Until then . . . then, when it's all clear . . . when all's clear . . . then,
why then

pearl your voice into my third, most watery
ear!
Here,
gather and gather
your shine into a wad
of spitfire light! Slalom
down my tunnels towards
the deep dark poetries
of a blood wedding.
Wait there. Wait.
Wait. *No me*
Fuye!
Stay.

Stay I say!

Wait until the leader clears the lunar.
Wait until, hip to hip,
arm rod-like against arm,
the eyes have it.

What is this thing called?

A Prelude to a Kiss

Under the water's skin
the mouth
is a handkerchief
sponging wet salts
that   wake   wonder.

Is this eye spilling
despair, or just
answering
to smoke, old age,
a stray   grain   of sand?

Anemone. Anemone.

*

The mouth
is a fist
full of fingers.
Soft teeth drift
in the deep.

A sea-rose,
licked pink,
turns purple
in cobalt's
icy blue.

Below the meniscus, things float:
                    fingers,
                    hands, cheek
                    bones.
No push.   No pull.   No current.

Only water
brushing a herd of medusas.
Thick things—   soft things,
smoothed
                  by water.

Smoother
still,
petals spread in
wet, unmetered
breath.

Anemone. Anemone.

                    *

Feeding on
each other's names,
the mouth
drowns, alleatoric,
in the eye.

Anonynominehmen'aimenescianomali,
Neumannamnesiasinenomonemesistema,

Stameneenenymphominimaliaminanemone,
Moanimomaterailymitimimesimillenaria

anemonstrosillypsistah, nomemataminemonoméme
simazisomyomendimensio.Dominamanimane

monodimelomaniamudiwamnesimilitude.
Anemonephylumcnidariacoelenteratantho

zoanematocyst.Anonymanemono
mi me nominanemone.

Anemone.
Anemone.

My Funny Valentine

after Miles Davis

I.

- Is your figure
  less than Greek?
  Is your mouth
  a little weak
  when you open
  it to speak? Are you smart?

- Long live Parmenides!

- Parmenides is dead.

II.

Hellas is fallen. *Hélas.*
The body decays as surely as earth's steam
draws all things into it. *Selah.*

What more is there to say?
A man on a horse went up the mountain
to see what he could see.

That much we've heard before.
The word on the street is
"Yes is yes. No is no."

And now a cavalry of one demands
that we find a new word for our time.
Stay. Among these collapsing columns

I am alone, and fogged in.
You are you. I am myself.
What else is there to say?

Small Consolation

for Jacques Coursil

Accordingly, Migran slips under lintels and into
other small places. The mangrove plays rope to
Migritude's hook: "No!"
Infantile speech and such. The succor, nothing but *sucre*,
trickles through *quand-même.* A babble of percolating
Counter Tobaccanism. Structurally,
> The House is in tact.
> It is just that the *veranda* (that is, The Court) is open.
> And this is where the real
> is lived. Or such was the case.

All of this assumes that you take his word (*Per se*). Anabasically,
trade four for four. *Fa,* the fourth, hovers *entre so et do*
until
> blue's gravity is forgotten,
> progress abandoned, and
> discourse assumed.

La chute, sûrement, ne t'interesse plus, at this late date.
Star apples etc. Layin down the tracks, on the other hand . . .
So intractably we come back to this question of
> whether the cat is in the box
> or the box is in the shredded cat,
> given that it is black. Likewise, the
> dreaded dog is dying out
> generation by generation. Wood foot, they say.
> More specifically, *le conte* romanizes itself,
> despite our beloved Cesar's municipal functions.

Con/sequently Migran takes it all with a grain of salt.
Condiments are always served at the table so that one
may pique whatever interests one. If this is lost
        in trans/*la*/*ti*/ *o* it may simply be that
        la boxe n'a rien à voir avec the box.
        Until one takes off one's gloves
        and writes back a daughter

Conjugation: To France
        From France
        Of France
        For France

Prepositionally speaking, this is of little
consequence. Furthermore it is all speculative,
a grammar of sorts. Oh, the Philologues!

It may be that that woman in the picture on the mantle
is his sister, wife, Sara, Claire, mistress, whatnot.
In any case, that is not under discussion.

All I saw was an envelope,
the thing you put things in,
or shred. Just call it a box.
This much is not up for debate.

L'angoisse du chat de Schrödinger did not
come up in that discussion. What upset us was
the frantic yowl of dancing cardboard,
as if possessed by a primitive drumbeat.
Yes, primitive. That is what
made us uncomfortable.

Our Embrace

for Franklin, after Brancusi

is monumental, a bloc representing
the phalanx that is us. Tending towards each,
other than the word our communal well utters,
we envision silence singly. This one sense is
our plenty, a sense of more than common sense.
G-d helped us, one might say, were misprision
not, in its own house, taken for language.
Our tongue in common remains unknown to
the greater world, we bound this region
true to our word, braced for the impact of
wind, dust, time, force, removal.
Schooled hard, we hold fast, and this
is the unrushed sense that speeds us
into each other, where we intend
to rest. It's true, it gives us pause.
Metallicized, it presents us, *Eia!,*
with all we did not need to make in
order to be here all along. Sandstone
is not specified; boulder overstates this
plain monument to the two in one, now us.

CARNAVAL.

Carnaval: A Suite[1]

The piano originated in Africa.
    —Abdullah Ibrahim[2]

I sit with Shakespeare and he winces not. Across the color-line I move arm in arm with Balzac and Dumas, where smiling men and welcoming women glide in gilded halls. From out the caves of the evening that swing between the strong-limbed earth and the tracery of the stars, I summon Aristotle and Aurelius and what soul I will, and they come all graciously with no scorn nor condescension.
    —W. E. B. Du Bois[3]

---

1. The poems in this sequence are inspired by Robert Schumann's Opus 9 *Carnaval: Scènes mignonnes sur quatres notes für das Pianoforte.*
2. Abdullah Ibrahim, "The World of Dollar: The Piano Originated in Africa" in *Cape Herald*, 19 October, 1968, 4.
3. W. E. B. Du Bois *The Souls of Black Folk* (Chicago: McClurg, 1903).

Préambule.

These have been the days
I wished to break like a stick
across my own knees, to splinter the
joy that took me. **Because it was not my own.**

Listen, listen!

*One time, there was rain that came after we prayed. We had learned
thirst's fervor swilling mouthfuls of sand. We danced a rain dance, and then
the rainfall came. It fell back to the earth.*

*Another time, I fingered a heart culled from my own herd, a cattle globe
whose valves leaked into my palm. In the lines of crisscrossed blood I read a
future that blurred out the mothers' tantrums, like bones tossed by a n'anga.*

To those who believe a flood is a spiritual thing,
preceded by tonguèd winds: **Be ashamed.**
It comes creeping up on you like
a snare . . . lightly, lightly
loosening the soil's death rattle. And then you are washed away

in the rain's rush.

Listen. Listen.

Pierrot.

Under the bridge there are
stones growing
smooth with the
slippage of water
                    and the
                smear campaign of silt.
The moon floats
                closer
        and closer,
                dragging below the bridge.

        Is it time
        or a limpid ripple
        of maize-silk swimming?
        And while we look away

        she glides under
        to the other side.

Light.

Arlequin.

And you thought I was coming
dressed in a three-corner hat
with bells and pastel diamonds
to tell jokes and reminisce about the
WhenWe's over tea and crumpets . . .
Please!

and i came in a black-front, red-back,
eye-whites rolled-back Fela juju suit
and told jokes bout how i sent you back to
yo old country lookin
like a howlin dog an
cryin fo the
po/lice.

Eusebius.

July's lessons:

the brevity of days,
the felling of trees,
the folly of light.

how nakedness lingers,
yet bears no embrace—
as if frost might make liars of us all.

the ice, implacable as quartz,
marks time while we seethe.
all is unchanged.

lateness blooms.
how is it that water spills
without spreading?

Florestan (aka Anikulapo).

Starting at full speed was what did it, mother-propelled, playing
with sticks and eyes and matches and guzzling tea, it all became
an inflammable glue, and I saw the tormented crowds were left
waiting, a multitude too dazed to make noise. So I started racing
towards them, only they were a sightless throng, and the old ones
were wearing embroidery and propped-up on wood canes, and the
five-year-olds, already coquettish, stretched dimpled arms towards
me begging god-knows-what while the uncles advised ad nauseum.

The glitter's glare confused them, the short shorts, the shekere
vamps so long so shuffle so shufferin so shmiley, and catching the
glint in their brassy eyes, I knew I should run but I had already
started at full speed, yet not really because I felt myself growing
faster, louder, a terrible shift in trapezoid mirrors. There were
lines, beautiful Euclidian curves, slipping their smooth arcs
across my thighs, my cheeks, my painted perfect body as I played
my two horns in one mouth, a cigarette, a hoarse, but I no be
gentleman at all!

And I say:
The frumpery of responsible women must end.   *(Ashé)*
The indigo beans of night are Truth.   *(Ashé)*
The garnet of cut skin is worse.   *(Ashé)*
Children will scream in church.   *(Ashé)*
Coated ones,
bearded men,
opulent ladies,
crocs, cowboys, and iron ladies,
the beastly, and the hastily praised
will be put in the stocks.

(Ashé)(Ashé) A.S.C.H.

I regret that I have been forced to flee the shooshing, shushing, embarrassed hushing of your too-strong concerns. I refuse to go up in flames. You will Ransome me. I may go out like a spent cigarette, my dear sarcophagus, but rest assured, I will return. Kalakuta.

Coquette.

Strange, how you bulge, Fish, ogling me down.
You are made of stillness, her actual substance,

yet your flitting tail speeds you away from me
into the vastness of your watery cage.

Fondness is like a jackhammer against the city's walkway.
Fondness pounds the glass into stagnant time, a cataclysmic and
    insistent finger.

Strangely you float, somewhere
beneath the weight of a meniscus, like

a long-lost water horse, serrating
the water with your gaping mouth.

Naartje and mango-green,
you swerve against the surface.

When do you get hungry? When do you drink?
Why do you never hurry, never wag, never answer

when I call your name?

Replique.

Strangely you loom, Finger, like the stench
of October before the earth unwraps herself to rain.

How slow and how sudden your fleshy approach,
as if only the last moment announced your impulse.

Into these tropics you come, anxious for adventure
turquoise and electric yellow. Then you fumble for a souvenir

I will not give.
I will not give.

I will not give.
You have the sand, and I, this gray-green gravel.

You have sun, and I, this fluorescence.
You have coral, and I, this oily glass,

filthy with your imprint.
I will not give.

Sphynxes.

for Cecil Taylor

tsssssssssssssssss.
szzzzzzzzzzzzzzzzzz.

shshshshshshshshshshshshshshsh.
zhzh zhzh zh zh zh zhzh zhhhhhhhhhhhhhhhh. (Hisssssssssssss.)

fffffffffffffffffff -ftssm- phph phph ph ph ph ph phph phph ph ph ph ph
PFEEEEEEEEEeeeeeeeeeeeeeee. (phyephophum) fix. kiss. nix.
tsk. tsk. tskskskskskskskskskskskskskskskksks.
sez Hisssssssssssssssss.
zhzhzhzhzhzhzhzh zhhhhhhhhhhhhhhhh
shooshooshooshooshshooshshoosh

szzzzzzzzzzzzzzzzzz.
Tsssssssssssssss.
Tststststststs!
ts ts.
ts.

Papillons.

Da capo al signo:
Look on, you greedy night moths,
and learn what comes of flying too close to the Flame.
Consider the mounded ash: how the wings
      once wore their silks so haughtily.

※

Well then, let's play blind as a bat,
fumbling awkwardly at daubs of color.
Let's be helpless and get stared at
like moths against the windowpane.

Who'll go first?
Who'll call "Hey!"
Then have to mutter, "You're not who I thought you were."
Why don't we wing it, like night owls in broad daylight?

I don't know much, and
even less I know is good.
But wouldn't you rather stumble with me
than hobble on your lonesome—bent heavy over a stick?

Lettres dansantes.

Eating flowers is quieter—
nasturtiums and sewing
and sweet solitude. The sanctity
of changing rooms—gawkish
in a chlorined corner—
or the mix of ballet: resin,
and sweat, and, self.
Eucalyptus—
briskly bruised.
Estrella, all I never
said about the
softness of her hands. Her
thrall—the satined cover.
How she fought off her
father. The flowering.

Chiarina.

for Yvonne Vera

Spun solipsisms loosened the eyetongue:
the ruling rooster would be unable

$$[F(\textit{th})/\mathrm{Br}/\mathrm{ggg}]$$

to decode a pile of butterfly
ashes.

Some things have no reason.   They choke.
Over and over again,   they choked
        them, thistled and thornlike.
        They came here.
They spindled and starved them out,
        dewbroke and dangled.

Achh well, it's just the widening gyre and gimble, no?

$$F[(\textit{th})\ \tfrac{1}{3}]B$$

No.

Over and over again,
we will stare down a narrow mine shaft
searching for our faces, as if in
        a water well built of stones,
        a well run dry.

Chopin.

Polish Sebastian.
Frenchified Fryderyk.
Sandy-sweet Boy Georges.
Nocturnal improv.
Delacroix brushstroke.
Puritan piano.

Or something   like that.

Estrella.

It occurs to me
that
maybe

I misunderstood her speech
                              and she mistook my hands.

   : Stars shot dead and reflective in a night pond are not near as dead as this.

Each wind musters old scent, sadness that has nothing to do with this,
sadness I haven't gotten around to. The pleated brown skirts, the dried
proteas, training to break the Guinness World Record for stair-climbing
with Nicky until he got hit by a car, my aunties (the one who went blind
and the one who did not), yes the Gogos. The African pastels of bauhinia
trees. Water, not holy water, drowning water, like his. Maybe every
baptism will be like this now. For tears, nine years too late. Nine years
too early. Sadness is a deep urn, full of something heavier than amber.

May be
                              each night
I will hear her speech   and she will feel my fingers.
                              for an age
She will feel my fingers   and I will hear her speech
                              each night

and it will keep occurring
to me
that

perhaps I misunderstood her and she mistook me.

   : Stars riding slipshod down two water towers, two cheeks far apart.

Reconnaissance.

after Hegel

MAKE A CHAIR. THEN BREAK IT ACROSS HIS BACK.
IF HE IS STILL STANDING HE WILL SOON FALL TO HIS KNEES.

Pantalon et Colombine.

Of dirty old men gunning down chicory coffee in the same crusted shirt
morning in, morning out.   Ogling
                                     the canteen girl
                                     (*Despina/Colombine*),
                                     with goat-eyes.

Of how such men pick through the ashtray
pilfering old butts, the pettiest of parsimonies.

Of how their stale thoughts ever shudder
across their flies and wandering thoughts: I'd like
                                       to teach her
                                       a thing or two.
                                       About this life or the next?

Of how the girls get younger every year, but the hype never flatlines.
Of how to cure the disease without a name by finding a toddler niece's
                                               pantyline.

Of how your odious little cigarette-barrel
                          (yes you, vakomana, I'm talking to you)
dangles between your legs, and
how it will never again do you a lick of good.
                                        Fuck you.

Valse Allemande.

Knit from these worms for a cap in the winter
this knotty new worsting of onyx and opal
is nevertheless wearing thin in some places—
a smooth and dark rock oiled with time surges through.

Anemone, windflower snatching the deep-horse.
Anemone, tenderly order is savaged.

The dreadful, the serpent, the charmer, the boxing.
The proteas drying to felt as to sandstone.

There is no blooming that comes without sting.
No spore can spawn it's own current, it's wind.

Paganini.

Pretty won't cut it, you gotta have flash.

Aveu.

And if you asked, what could I say?
"Before you knew me, I was abstract"?

I was one to wander alone, waiting for the city to exceed
her limits, while the ring-road rusted to earth-ochered red.

I could tell you about acacia trees. Their solitude thrashes
against the horizon, a mess of pods sung empty.

I could tell you how comfortless kerosene smells. Water steaming
in a keening pot, and everything so dark you forget it.

I could tell you elaborate lies about jacaranda neon crushed underfoot,
about killing-bees blamed on the wind, the crowd, and the pre-rain sun.

I could tell you that the night's ceiling is so overcharged with precious stones
that not even a rabid dog dares woo the Pearl back to earth.

And still I would have no answer.
Perhaps it is better for you never to know.

Promenade.

In the second year of the golden quarter
a body slipped over our own
although we had not known it since the first of the stone virgin dances.
It carved across the laughter and
razed with cubist ire all that had been evident.

This was how the aftertaste of
whitened manganese returned,
as we recalled the golden wilt of maize,
the empty glint of rice grains
and the absent-minded bread.

At that time sugar was a bitter joke,
flour pointless, oil a stinging insult.
We began haunting *muzhanje* trees,
and crazy schemes like wild lupine greens.
We shut up about the lost days,
the flame trees, the outdoor rugs,
unclassified herds, and smoking thunder.
These also became things to hoard.

And we watched, stunned at neighbors
turning hunger into coinage.
Rude profit soiled everyone's hands.
There was less clasping.

You know, we had heard of places
where such things were not uncommon,
bribes to grease a barrow-wheel, or ink
the commission-stamp. But we
were not like that. We never boasted

of damask, or gold, or libraries lost in sand.
All we had were calloused hands, and now callous minds.

This body came and waited
in spite of the Grand Measures Board.
It simply hooded its roosting eyes
and watched from a distance, malingering.

Pause. (For All the Madibas)

There is a breath before the pendulum rends its center,
a breath before what leapt comes back to its ground.

There, men and women in chains broke rock, forcing it to deliver

                   silence.

Hours on end, for year after year
of gravel's grating humiliation,
men and women, clay-footed,
sat with Shakespeare.
They were never shamed.
May their memories be forever

                   blessed.

Marche des Davidsbündler contre les Philistins.

(for my countrymen who lived below average, gone at forty-four)

I want you! men who have grown crimson noses and other debaucheries.
I want you! women who have crocheted your hair and smoked your voices.
Let these be my soothsayers.

How many municipal tiles smothered the legend?
Tag the city wall once more, O you the never browbeatens!
Take up your spray-canned friezes, O you the true heroics!

Turn in your graves, if you are soft-hearted,
or shift in your seats, Alsatians. Boldness wields no magic but brevity.
A louver this way and a louver that way is a louver all the same.

I want you! eternally betrothed, unable to mourn in the cornfields.
I want you! mothers cursed with long life, with graves too small to visit.
Let these by my timekeepers.

How strange, that the mirror should be a window,
the gum tree, a eucalyptus,
and I,　　　　　the slighting lover.

Turn in your graves, you African Methodists.
For this will a man leave his father and mother.
For this he returns, and for this she ran.

Give me bread when I hunger,
Let me choke on meatless soups,
Let me cry, cry for water,
Let me long for looks not stares.

She knew how, at the least,
To mold elemental caskets,
To count those dead from overloving,
And bargain with the morgues.

I want you! arms pocked like cheeks with the bruising butt of visions.
I want you! lungs of tar filled with new consumptive lurking.
Let these be my only band of angels.

I am crossing. Tomorrow I go and who knows but that I will not return.
I am crossing city loudness the moon dimmer, the ancestral mute.
There I will face the battle of the dwindle,
                              leprosy exiled on the Island of Seals
                              a surf washing me away from myself
There I will face the ocean's greed, I will mirror it. I will master it. I will window it.
It will pass   *through me.*
Who knows but that I will return.

I call you, my soothsayers, my keepers, my angels,
to toast my good fortune endlessly.
On the wrong ocean, peaceful, I will wait and wait
for the weight of my error to show itself
and the bones the bones the old bones
to wash up on this other side.

Gabriela! Mistral!   :   let none find me abstruse.
I have spoken of Goethe, trade spoils, and a disease we dare not name.
I have called upon your conjunction, that meeting of the two southernmost waters.
I have known that he and I will love again,
                         in memories
                              yet never live as in
                              the days of cruel good
                              fortune. O stung, O
                              stung:

HOW IS IT POSSIBLE THAT WATER SPILLS,
YET CANNOT SPREAD?

Liturgy

Grant, O God, that when I return
I will remember the language of my bunionned grandmother
Rolling towards me to run her rough hands up and down my arms.

Grant that the soles of my feet
Will still be thick enough to smother the flames of October suns
That toast the rain-grass a crisp crunching gold.

Grant that my eyes
Will water each time I see a musasa's new leaves
Blushing for arriving just a little before spring.
Let them stay dry in the smoke of the kitchens
So round and so dark with no power kumusha.

Grant that I will remember
The names of my cattle, who I won as a
A six-year-old too stubborn to believe
That Sekuru could give to my brother but not me.
Grant, Mwari Above All Else,
That I will be able to swallow the soup
Of my ancestors as I chew
On the slaughtered liver, and hear their
Voices in an empty pod—
Cowbell sounds of the mbira huru.

Grant that I will not notice
The scented comrades, crammed in
A fuming cooperative bus, but instead
Breathe in the mists of head-balanced baskets
Stuffed with ripe mangoes, maize, fowl, groundnuts.

Grant that I will not get lost
But instead, like a sleepwalker blind but sure
Stride through grey labyrinths, down
Township paths. Let me find the concrete prism houses
Where my aunt lived her last days and left me my cousins.

Grant, O One Who Takes No Name,
That I will answer when they call me
Tsitsi, Madhuve,
Musikana wemazvimbakupa
Muzukuru, Mainini, Muninina,
Daughter of the soil,
Daughter of the soil,
Stay with us awhile.

To Bless the Memory of Tamir Rice

Plant twelve date palms in a ring around the tarmac. Make them
tall, slight towers, leaning into the wind as princes do. Fear that
the sweetness of dates will churn your stomach. Plant them anyways.

Plant the pudge of his fuzzless face in the arrested time of a school portrait.
Plant his exotic name—found in a book that spelled dreams
of eminence and hope for an uncertain coupling—in your ear.

Know that whether it leaches into the soil or not, this ground
was watered with his blood. This tarmac turned a rioting red. Strike that.
There was a screech of brakes, and sirens howling like a cliché, then

a volley of pops that might have been a game if only
what came next was not such utter silence.
The tarmac was red. There was no riot.

Build a circle of palms and something to keep them safe.
Build a greenhouse around the twelve palms.
Yes, a green house. This land is not our land.

Dig up the tarmac, the dark heavy loam of this side of town.
Be sure to wear gloves as you dig through the brownfield's
mystification. Once the Cuyahoga River was a wall of fire.

God knows how rain melts metal.
Dig into that earth and build
a foundation. Quarry it.

Let the little boys and little girls of Shaker Heights and Orange
bring a Game Boy or cellphone, or other toy made out of coltan that,
chances are, a little boy or little girl dug up by hand in the DRC.

Let the children lay their shiny toys in the foundation.
Seal up ground with molten lead. Die-cast its melted weight.
Yes, make a typecaster's mold, and leave it a dull grey, like flint.

Stamp out a broadside, only set it in the foundation's floor.
Let us read the letter that says this officer was unfit.
Let us go over it step by step, every time we walk toward the green

house of imagining what this boy's boyhood should have been,
the fulfilling of his name, his promise.
Plant an oasis here. How is not my problem.

*

Let someone who remember how cook de rice.
Let she cook de rice with palm oil 'til is yellow an sticky.
Of course dem have palm oil in Cleveland. Dis no Third World we livin in.

Let she cook she rice an peas. Let she say
how she know to do it from a film she seen. In de film, dem people from
de sea island gone to Sierra Leone and dema find dey people,

dey people dat sing de same song with de same words. Come to
find out dem words is not jes playplay words, dem words for weeping. So dema
sit down together, an weep together, dey South Carolina an Sierra Leone family.

Dey weep over de war, an de water, an de fresh and de forgotten,
an dey cook dat rice 'til is yellow and sticky. Dey nyam it with dey hand,
outta banana leaf and de old, old man, him say,

you never forget the language you cry in.

Let all dem little girls from Shaker Heights skip the gymnastics meet.
Let dem come and eat rice and eat rice 'til they don't want to eat rice no more
an let dem still have rice to eat. Let them lose their innocence.

Let horizons settle low.
Let dates and raisins and apples and nuts seem a strange mockery
of the new, the sweet, the hoped for. Let us share the matter.

Let us sit here under these date palms,
and haggle over whose fault it is. Let the rage that says tear this shit down
tear this shit down.

Let us start with the glass walls of the greenhouse, as a demonstration.
Let the rage that says I cannot speak not speak.
Let it suck speech into its terrible maw and leave us shuddering in silence.

Let the rage that says, black lives matter matter.
Let that other rage that says all lives matter be torn down. Let the matter with how
we don't all matter in the same way churn up a monumental penitence.

Let the date palm offer us shade.
Let us ask why we are still here.
Let us lower our eyes as we face his mother, his father, his sister.

ACKNOWLEDGMENTS

Some of the poems in this collection were first published elsewhere, as listed below.

The Book of VaNyemba in *Jalada*

"Praise Song for Patricia Jabbeh Wesley" in *Prairie Schooner*

"Song of Yobe" and "Matobo Hills" on *Poetry International's* Zimbabwe page

"To Praise the Hornbill" in *Madison Review*

Family Trees and portions of *Carnaval: A Suite* in my chapbook *Carnaval* in *Seven New Generation African Poets: A Chapbook Box Set*

"Dust to Dust" in *Bitter Oleander*

"Deep English" and "Document" in *InTensions*

"Blunt Balm" in *ElevenEleven*

"Sign: Wait Until the Leader Clears the Lunar" in *Elsewhere*

"Liturgy" in *Runes Review*

I am profoundly grateful to Kwame Dawes, Chris Abani, Gabeba Baderoon, Bernardine Evaristo, John Keene, Matt Shenoda, and all of the poets they have brought into my life through the African Poetry Book Fund. I thank Micere Mugo, Dwayne Betts, Patricia Smith, VONA and Diem Jones, Keorapetse Kgositsile, Bob Perelman, Herman Beavers, Taije Silverman, Joe Donahue, and Nate Mackey for their encouragement along the way. I thank my family for their endless inspiration, and I beg their forgiveness for spilling the beans.

NOTES

THE BOOK OF VANYEMBA

Ex nihilo, omnia.: "Out of the void comes all." (The Beginning)

Plorans ploravit in nocte.: "She weeps bitterly through the night." (Lamentations 1:2)

Virgines eius squalidæ, et ipsa oppressa amaritudine.: "Her young women grieve, and she is in bitter anguish." (Lamentations 1:4)

Alia autem ceciderunt in petrosa, ubi non habebant terram multam.: "Some fell on rocky places, where there was not much earth." (Matthew 13:5)

Benedictus fructus ventris tui.: "Blessed is the fruit of your womb." (Luke 1:42)

Esurivi enim, et dedistis mihi manducare.: "For I was hungry and you gave me food." (Matthew 25:35)

Eli, Eli, lamma sabacthani? hoc est: Deus meus, Deus meus ut quid dereliquisti me?: "Eli, Eli, lama sabachthani?" that is, "My God, My God, why have You forsaken Me?" (Matthew 27:46)

Oculi tui columbarum, absque eo, quod intrinsecus latet.: "You have doves' eyes hidden behind your locks." (Song of Songs 4:1)

99

After the Ceremonies:
New and Selected Poems
Ama Ata Aidoo
Edited and with a foreword
by Helen Yitah

The Promise of Hope: New and
Selected Poems, 1964–2013
Kofi Awoonor
Edited and with an introduction
by Kofi Anyidoho

The January Children
Safia Elhillo

Madman at Kilifi
Clifton Gachagua

Beating the Graves
Tsitsi Ella Jaji

Gabriel Okara: Collected Poems
Gabriel Okara
Edited and with an introduction
by Brenda Marie Osbey

The Kitchen-Dweller's Testimony
Ladan Osman

Fuchsia
Mahtem Shiferraw

Logotherapy
Mukoma Wa Ngugi

When the Wanderers Come Home
Patricia Jabbeh Wesley

Seven New Generation African
Poets: A Chapbook boxed set
Edited by Kwame Dawes
and Chris Abani
(Slapering Hol)

Eight New-Generation African
Poets: A Chapbook Box Set
Edited by Kwame Dawes
and Chris Abani
(Akashic Books)

New-Generation African Poets:
A Chapbook Box Set (Tatu)
Edited by Kwame Dawes
and Chris Abani
(Akashic Books)

New-Generation African Poets:
A Chapbook Box Set (Nne)
Edited by Kwame Dawes
and Chris Abani
(Akashic Books)

To order or obtain more information on these or other University of
Nebraska Press titles, visit nebraskapress.unl.edu. For more information
about the African Poetry Book Series, visit africanpoetrybf.unl.edu.

CPSIA information can be obtained
at www.ICGtesting.com
Printed in the USA
LVOW11s0235060117
519889LV00003B/244/P